BEYOND TOMORROW

Escaping the grip of procrastination

Shawn V. Orr

INTRODUCTION

Welcome to the book "Beyond Tomorrow: Escaping the Grip of Procrastination." Procrastination's pull can be overwhelming in a world full with chances and never-ending tasks, impeding both professional and personal development. This book serves as a guide to help you uncover the hidden causes of procrastination and equip yourself with the necessary skills to overcome it.

We will explore the psychology of procrastination on the pages that follow, figuring out why we put off crucial chores and the consequences for our lives. This trip is a blueprint for productivity and long-term transformation, not merely an investigation of the issue.

You will learn how to turn procrastination into productive behaviour by comprehending the thinking of the procrastinator, identifying the cycles of delay, and identifying practical solutions.

TABLE OF CONTENTS

CHAPTER ONE

Understanding Procrastination

The deliberate delay or postponement of activities, even with the knowledge that such delays may have unfavourable effects, is the hallmark of procrastination, a complicated behavioural phenomena. There is a disconnect between purpose and action in this situation, as people put off important chores in favour of more enjoyable and instantaneous pursuits.

Procrastination is caused by a number of psychological factors:

1. Cognitive Factors: One common cause of procrastination is faulty thinking, such as overestimating the effort or underestimating the amount of time needed to complete a task. Unrealistic expectations are a result of cognitive biases such as the planning fallacy.

2. Emotional Drivers: Fears of success or failure, worry, and self-doubt are a few examples of emotions that have a big impact on put off tasks. People may choose to put off chores that make them feel bad in favour of immediate gratification over long-term objectives.

3. Temporal Discounting: People have a propensity to value instant gratification above delayed benefits. A propensity to prioritise immediate gratification over the long-term effects of postponing chores can lead to procrastination.

4. Fear and Anxiety: People who are afraid of failing can become paralysed and reluctant to start tasks. Conversely, anxiety about greater obligations and expectations can result from a fear of success.

5. Self-Regulation and Willpower: Procrastination is a result of weak self-control and willpower. People could find it difficult to stay focused, turn away from distractions, and follow schedules.

6. Perfectionism: Aiming for perfection might cause people to put off work because they fear that they won't live up to their extremely high standards. Project launch and completion may be unrealistically hampered by this fastidious mentality.

7. Task Avoidance and Psychological Resistance: One common way that people who procrastinate avoid unpleasant or difficult jobs is by doing so. A subconscious defence mechanism against discomfort or uncertainty may appear as psychological resistance.

8. Motivational Factors: One of the main causes of procrastination is low motivation, which can stem from a lack of interest or a false sense of the importance of a work. Retaining motivation over time becomes essential to overcoming setbacks.

9. Individual Variations: Procrastination tendencies are influenced by personality qualities like impulsivity, conscientiousness, and self-efficacy. Customising successful techniques requires an understanding of these individual distinctions.

A multifaceted strategy is needed to address procrastination, including cognitive restructuring, emotion regulation, time management techniques, and developing intrinsic drive. Through a thorough analysis of the psychological foundations of procrastination, people may create plans to deal with and eventually overcome this prevalent issue, leading to a more successful and meaningful life.

Identifying Procrastination Triggers

Understanding and addressing procrastination requires a keen awareness of the specific triggers that prompt individuals to delay tasks. Procrastination triggers can vary widely among individuals, but recognizing them is a crucial step toward developing effective coping strategies. Here are key aspects to consider:

1. Task-Related Triggers:

-Task Difficulty: Tasks perceived as overly complex or challenging may trigger procrastination. Breaking them down into smaller, manageable steps can alleviate this trigger.

-Lack of Clarity: Unclear instructions or vague goals can lead to confusion and hesitation. Clearly defining tasks and setting specific objectives helps reduce ambiguity.

2. Emotional Triggers:

-Fear of Failure or Success: Fear can be a powerful trigger for procrastination. The fear of not meeting expectations (failure) or the fear of increased responsibilities (success) may hinder initiation.

-Anxiety: High levels of anxiety, whether related to a task or external factors, can contribute to procrastination. Identifying sources of anxiety and implementing stress management techniques is essential.

3. Temporal Triggers:

-Deadline Proximity: Some individuals thrive under pressure, leading them to procrastinate until a deadline is imminent. Understanding one's relationship with deadlines can help in planning and time management.

4. Environmental Triggers:

- **Distractions:** Environmental factors, such as noise, clutter, or interruptions, can act as triggers. Creating a conducive work environment minimizes potential distractions.

-Proximity to Temptations: Being close to enjoyable but non-essential activities (e.g., social media, entertainment) can tempt individuals away from tasks. Managing these temptations is crucial.

5. Motivational Triggers:

- **Lack of Interest:** A lack of intrinsic motivation due to disinterest in a task can trigger procrastination. Finding ways to make tasks more engaging or linking them to personal goals enhances motivation.

-Goal Misalignment: Tasks that are not aligned with personal or long-term goals may lack the necessary motivation for prompt completion. Regularly reassessing goals ensures alignment.

6. Personal Triggers:

-Perfectionism: The pursuit of perfection can be a trigger, as the fear of not meeting exceptionally high standards may lead to avoidance. Embracing a more realistic approach to tasks can counteract this trigger.

-Low Self-Efficacy: Doubts about one's ability to successfully complete a task can be a powerful trigger. Building self-efficacy through skill development and positive reinforcement is essential.

Identifying procrastination triggers involves self-reflection, observation, and an honest assessment of one's thought patterns and emotional responses. Once these triggers are recognized, individuals can proactively implement targeted strategies to mitigate their impact, ultimately fostering a proactive and productive approach to tasks.

CHAPTER TWO

The Procrastinator's mindset

Exploring Common Thought Patterns in Procrastination

Procrastination is intricately linked to thought patterns that can either propel individuals into action or perpetuate the cycle of delay. By delving into these common thought patterns, we gain insight into the cognitive aspects of procrastination and how they influence behavior:

1. Negative Self-Talk:

   - **Pattern:** Engaging in self-critical or defeatist inner dialogue.

   - **Impact:** Undermines self-confidence and creates a mental barrier to task initiation.

   - **Counteraction:** Practicing positive affirmations, reframing negative thoughts, and cultivating self-compassion.

2. Cognitive Distortions:

- **Pattern:** Adopting distorted or irrational thinking patterns.

- **Impact:** Contributes to skewed perceptions of tasks, making them seem more daunting or less achievable than they are.

- **Counteraction:** Cognitive restructuring techniques, such as identifying and challenging irrational thoughts, to promote more realistic perspectives.

3. Temporal Discounting:

- **Pattern:** Focusing excessively on immediate rewards rather than long-term consequences.

- **Impact:** Prioritizes short-term pleasure over long-term goals, leading to procrastination.

- **Counteraction:** Developing a future-oriented mindset, emphasizing the delayed but significant rewards of task completion.

4. Perfectionist Ideals:

- **Pattern:** Setting unrealistically high standards for oneself.

- **Impact:** Paralyzes action due to fear of not meeting perfectionist expectations.

- **Counteraction:** Embracing a mindset of progress over perfection, breaking tasks into smaller steps, and acknowledging achievements along the way.

5. Fear of Failure:

- **Pattern:** Anticipating negative outcomes and associating tasks with potential failure.

- **Impact:** Generates anxiety and avoidance behaviors.

- **Counteraction:** Adopting a growth mindset, reframing failure as a learning opportunity, and setting realistic expectations.

6. Overwhelmed Thinking:

- **Pattern:** Viewing tasks as insurmountable, leading to a sense of overwhelm.

- **Impact:** Provokes avoidance due to perceived task complexity.

- **Counteraction:** Breaking tasks into smaller, more manageable components, and creating a step-by-step plan for execution.

7. Decisional Procrastination:

- **Pattern:** Deliberating excessively on decisions, leading to delayed action.

- **Impact:** Hinders progress by keeping individuals stuck in the decision-making phase.

- **Counteraction:** Implementing decision-making strategies, setting deadlines for choices, and focusing on the benefits of making timely decisions.

Exploring and understanding these thought patterns is a crucial step in breaking the cycle of procrastination. By recognizing and challenging counterproductive cognitive habits, individuals can cultivate a more constructive mindset that fosters proactive and timely task completion.

OVERCOMING NEGATIVE BELIEFS

Overcoming negative beliefs is a pivotal aspect of combating procrastination and fostering personal growth. Negative beliefs, whether about oneself, tasks, or the world, can create mental barriers that contribute to the reluctance to take action. Here are key considerations for addressing and overcoming negative beliefs:

1. Identification:
- **Recognizing Negative Beliefs:** Start by identifying the negative beliefs that fuel procrastination. These may include thoughts about inadequacy, fear of failure, or doubts about one's abilities.

2. Challenge and Reframe:
- **Questioning Validity:** Challenge the validity of negative beliefs by questioning their accuracy and considering alternative, more constructive perspectives. Reframe negative thoughts into positive or neutral affirmations.

3. Self-Compassion:

- **Cultivating Self-Compassion:** Treat oneself with kindness and understanding. Acknowledge that everyone faces challenges and setbacks, and self-compassion can counteract the impact of negative beliefs.

4. Mindfulness Practices:

- **Staying Present:** Engage in mindfulness practices to stay present and focused. This helps in breaking the cycle of negative thoughts that often fuel procrastination.

5. Goal Setting and Achievements:

- **Setting Realistic Goals:** Establish realistic and achievable goals, celebrating small victories along the way. Positive experiences contribute to building a more positive self-image.

6. Positive Affirmations:

- **Affirming Positive Qualities:** Regularly affirm personal strengths and positive qualities. This fosters a mindset shift away from negative self-perceptions.

7. Seeking Support:

- Sharing with Others: Discuss negative beliefs with trusted friends, family, or mentors. External perspectives can offer valuable insights and support in challenging negative thought patterns.

8. Therapeutic Interventions:

- Professional Guidance: If negative beliefs persist, seeking the help of a therapist or counselor can provide targeted interventions to address underlying issues and facilitate positive change.

9. Learning and Growth Mindset:

- Embracing Growth: Cultivate a growth mindset that views challenges as opportunities for learning and growth. Embracing setbacks as part of the journey can diminish the impact of negative beliefs.

10. Visualization Techniques:

- Positive Imagery: Use visualization techniques to picture successful outcomes. Creating mental images of achieving goals can counteract negative beliefs and boost confidence.

This is an ongoing process that requires self-awareness, self-compassion, and intentional efforts to reshape thought patterns. By actively challenging and transforming negative beliefs, individuals can pave the way for a more positive and empowered approach to tasks, ultimately breaking free from the shackles of procrastination.

CHAPTER THREE

The procrastination cycle

The procrastination cycle is a recurring pattern of behavior characterized by the delay or avoidance of tasks, creating a loop that reinforces procrastination. Understanding the components of this cycle is crucial for breaking free from its grip:

1. Task Avoidance:

  - Initiation Hesitation: Procrastination often begins with hesitation in starting a task. Individuals may experience anxiety, uncertainty, or a lack of motivation that hinders the initial step.

2. Short-Term Relief:

  - Engaging in Distractions: Faced with the discomfort of task initiation, individuals turn to short-term, enjoyable distractions such as social media, entertainment, or other non-essential activities.

- Immediate Gratification: Engaging in these distractions provides a momentary sense of relief and pleasure, offering immediate gratification.

3. Increased Stress and Anxiety:

- Proximity to Deadlines: As the deadline approaches, the awareness of time running out intensifies stress and anxiety. The pressure to complete the task becomes more pronounced.

4. Last-Minute Rush:

- Forced Action: The mounting pressure forces individuals into action, often at the last possible moment. This rush may lead to suboptimal outcomes due to limited time for thoughtful planning and execution.

5. Negative Consequences:

- Subpar Results: Procrastination frequently results in subpar outcomes due to rushed efforts, reinforcing negative beliefs about one's capabilities.

- **Increased Stress Levels:** The stress and anxiety associated with the last-minute rush can have detrimental effects on mental and emotional well-being.

6. Post-Task Regret:

- **Reflecting on Delays:** After completing the task, individuals may reflect on the unnecessary stress caused by procrastination and regret not addressing the task earlier.

- **Pledging to Change:** A common response is to pledge to avoid procrastination in the future, initiating a cycle of motivation that may be short-lived.

Understanding this cycle is vital for interrupting the pattern of procrastination. Breaking the cycle involves addressing each stage strategically:

- **Task Initiation Strategies:** Implement techniques to overcome hesitation and initiate tasks, such as breaking them into smaller, more manageable steps.

- Distraction Management: Develop skills to manage distractions and create a focused work environment to reduce the temptation of immediate gratification.

- Time Management: Implement effective time management practices to distribute tasks evenly, reducing the reliance on last-minute rushes.

- Stress Reduction Techniques: Incorporate stress reduction techniques, such as mindfulness or regular breaks, to manage stress and anxiety throughout the task.

By dismantling the procrastination cycle through targeted interventions at each stage, individuals can cultivate habits that promote timely action and break free from the detrimental patterns associated with chronic procrastination.

CHAPTER FOUR

Procrastination pitfalls

Procrastination vs Productivity

Procrastination and productivity represent two opposing ends of the spectrum when it comes to task management and goal achievement. Understanding the dynamics between procrastination and productivity is essential for individuals seeking to enhance their efficiency and overall effectiveness:

1. Definition and Characteristics:

  - **Procrastination:** Involves delaying or postponing tasks, often due to avoidance of discomfort, fear of failure, or other psychological factors.

  - **Productivity:** Refers to the ability to efficiently complete tasks and achieve goals, making effective and timely use of one's time and resources.

2. Motivation and Action:

- **Procrastination:** Tends to be associated with a lack of motivation, leading to delayed or incomplete actions.

- **Productivity:** Thrives on motivation, with individuals actively taking steps to accomplish tasks in a timely manner.

3. Time Management:

- **Procrastination:** Often results in poor time management, with tasks piling up until imminent deadlines force action.

- **Productivity:** Involves effective time allocation, planning, and prioritization to ensure tasks are completed efficiently without unnecessary delays.

4. Quality of Work:

- **Procrastination:** May lead to rushed and subpar work quality due to last-minute efforts.

- **Productivity:** Emphasizes delivering high-quality work by distributing efforts evenly and allowing time for thorough planning and execution.

5. Stress and Anxiety:

- **Procrastination:** Increases stress and anxiety as deadlines approach, creating a cycle of heightened pressure.

- **Productivity:** Focuses on stress reduction by spreading tasks over time, allowing for a more manageable workload.

6. Goal Achievement:

- **Procrastination:** Hinders progress toward long-term goals due to delayed actions and missed opportunities.

- Productivity: Facilitates goal attainment by consistently working towards objectives, ensuring steady progress.

7. Mindset and Attitude:

- **Procrastination:** Often associated with a reactive mindset, addressing tasks only when urgency compels action.

- **Productivity:** Reflects a proactive mindset, where individuals take initiative and actively seek opportunities for improvement.

8. Learning and Growth:

- **Procrastination:** Limits learning opportunities and personal growth, as delayed actions may result in missed chances for development.

- **Productivity:** Encourages continuous learning and growth, fostering a mindset that embraces challenges and seeks improvement.

9. Self-Efficacy:

- **Procrastination:** Undermines self-confidence and belief in one's ability to successfully complete tasks.

- **Productivity:** Boosts self-efficacy by fostering a sense of accomplishment through consistent task completion.

10. Long-Term Impact:

- **Procrastination:** Can lead to a cycle of missed opportunities, increased stress, and unfulfilled potential.

- **Productivity:** Sets the stage for long-term success, satisfaction, and a sense of fulfillment through sustained effort and accomplishment.

Balancing the scales towards productivity involves cultivating effective time management habits, maintaining motivation, and adopting a proactive approach to tasks. By understanding the contrasts between procrastination and productivity, individuals can make intentional choices that align with their goals and contribute to a more fulfilling and successful life.

Consequences of chronic procrastination

Chronic procrastination can have a range of significant consequences that impact various aspects of an individual's life. Here are some key repercussions:

1. Missed Opportunities:

   - Chronic procrastination often results in missed opportunities, as delayed actions can lead to the expiration of deadlines or the inability to capitalize on favorable circumstances.

2. Decreased Performance:

- Continuous procrastination can lead to subpar performance due to rushed and last-minute efforts, impacting the quality of work and diminishing overall achievements.

3. Increased Stress and Anxiety:

- Procrastination contributes to heightened stress and anxiety, particularly as deadlines approach. The pressure of impending tasks can lead to chronic stress, negatively affecting mental well-being.

4. Strained Relationships:

- Delays in completing responsibilities may strain relationships, especially if others depend on timely actions. This can lead to misunderstandings, frustration, and a breakdown in trust.

5. Compromised Health:

- The stress associated with chronic procrastination can have physical consequences, including disrupted sleep,

increased blood pressure, and a compromised immune
system.

6. Negative Self-Image:

- Individuals who consistently procrastinate may
develop a negative self-image, eroding self-esteem and
self-confidence. Persistent feelings of guilt and
self-blame can further contribute to a diminished sense
of self-worth.

7. Career Implications:

- In a professional context, chronic procrastination can
hinder career advancement. Consistently missing
deadlines or producing subpar work may impact
opportunities for promotions and success.

8. Financial Consequences:

- Delayed actions may lead to financial consequences,
such as missed investment opportunities, late payments,
or the accrual of penalties and fees.

9. Impaired Learning:

- Students who procrastinate may experience impaired learning outcomes, as delayed studying and rushed assignments can compromise understanding and retention of material.

10. Loss of Motivation:
- Chronic procrastination can create a cycle of demotivation, making it increasingly challenging to find the drive to initiate and complete tasks.

11. Compromised Goal Achievement:
- Long-term goals may be compromised due to the cumulative effect of procrastination. Consistently delaying actions necessary for goal attainment can lead to unfulfilled aspirations.

12. Time Management Challenges:
- Chronic procrastination often indicates poor time management skills. Inability to effectively allocate time can perpetuate a cycle of delayed actions and heightened stress.

Addressing chronic procrastination requires a combination of self-awareness, effective time management strategies, and the development of proactive habits. Seeking support from mentors, coaches, or mental health professionals can be beneficial for individuals struggling to break free from the cycle of procrastination and its associated consequences.

CHAPTER FIVE

Strategies for immediate action

Strategies for immediate action are essential for overcoming procrastination and fostering a proactive approach to tasks. Here are effective techniques to prompt immediate action:

1. The Two-Minute Rule:

  - If a task takes less than two minutes to complete, do it immediately. This helps tackle small tasks promptly, preventing them from accumulating.

2. Create a To-Do List:

  - Outline tasks in a to-do list, breaking them down into smaller, manageable steps. Prioritize tasks and start with the most urgent or important ones.

3. Set Micro-Goals:

- Establish small, achievable goals for immediate action. Completing these micro-goals provides a sense of accomplishment and builds momentum for larger tasks.

4. Use Timers and Pomodoro Technique:

- Set a timer for a short period (e.g., 25 minutes) and focus solely on the task during that time. The Pomodoro Technique helps manage time effectively and prevents procrastination.

5. Eliminate Distractions:

- Create a focused work environment by minimizing distractions. Turn off notifications, close unnecessary tabs, and establish a dedicated space for tasks.

6. Visualize the End Result:

- Picture the positive outcome of completing the task. Visualization can motivate immediate action by emphasizing the benefits and rewards.

7. Start with the Easiest Task:

- Begin with a task that is easy or enjoyable. This initial success can boost confidence and make it easier to transition to more challenging tasks.

8. Use Positive Reinforcement:

- Reward yourself for completing tasks promptly. Positive reinforcement, whether small treats or breaks, can create a positive association with immediate action.

9. Accountability Partners:

- Share your goals with someone who can hold you accountable. Knowing that someone is aware of your intentions can provide motivation for immediate action.

10. Practice Mindfulness:

- Stay present in the moment and focus on the task at hand. Mindfulness techniques, such as deep breathing, can help reduce anxiety and promote immediate action.

11. Commit to Five Minutes:

- Tell yourself you'll work on the task for just five minutes. Often, once you start, you'll find it easier to continue beyond the initial timeframe.

12. Break Down Tasks:

- Divide larger tasks into smaller, more manageable components. Addressing these smaller parts makes the overall task less daunting and encourages immediate action.

13. Establish a Routine:

- Incorporate tasks into a daily routine. Consistency helps form habits, making it more likely to initiate actions promptly.

14. Change Your Environment:

- Move to a different location if you find yourself stuck in a procrastination loop. A change in environment can provide a fresh perspective and stimulate action.

15. Reflect on Consequences:

- Consider the consequences of not taking immediate action. Reflecting on the negative outcomes of procrastination can motivate swift responses.

Experiment with these strategies to identify what works best for you. Combining multiple techniques can create a personalized approach to prompt immediate action and overcome procrastination.

CHAPTER SIX

Overcoming procrastination habits

Overcoming procrastination habits involves adopting effective strategies and cultivating a proactive mindset. Here are actionable steps to help you break free from the cycle of procrastination:

1. Self-Reflection:

- Identify the underlying reasons for procrastination. Understand your patterns, triggers, and the specific tasks that commonly lead to delays.

2. Set Clear Goals:

- Define clear and achievable goals. Break them down into smaller, manageable tasks with specific deadlines. Clarity in your objectives can make it easier to initiate action.

3. Prioritize Tasks:

- Prioritize tasks based on urgency and importance. Tackling high-priority tasks first helps prevent them from becoming sources of procrastination.

4. Create a Schedule:

- Develop a daily or weekly schedule outlining when specific tasks will be addressed. A structured routine provides a framework for consistent productivity.

5. Use Time Management Techniques:

- Employ time management techniques such as the Pomodoro Technique, time blocking, or the Eisenhower Matrix to allocate time effectively and maintain focus.

6. Break Tasks into Smaller Steps:

- Divide larger tasks into smaller, more manageable steps. This makes the overall task less overwhelming and increases the likelihood of taking immediate action.

7. Establish Deadlines:

- Set realistic deadlines for tasks. Having a timeframe creates a sense of urgency and can motivate you to start working on the task sooner.

8. Eliminate Distractions:

- Minimize potential distractions by turning off notifications, creating a dedicated workspace, and managing interruptions during focused work periods.

9. Positive Affirmations:

- Replace negative self-talk with positive affirmations. Affirmations can help reshape your mindset, boost confidence, and reduce the fear associated with tasks.

10. Visualize Success:

- Visualize yourself successfully completing tasks. This positive imagery can reinforce the motivation needed to overcome procrastination.

11. Accountability Partners:

- Share your goals with someone who can hold you accountable. Regular check-ins with a friend, colleague, or mentor can provide external motivation.

12. Reward Yourself:

- Establish a system of rewards for completing tasks. Celebrate small victories to reinforce positive behavior and create a positive association with productivity.

13. Address Perfectionism:

- Recognize and challenge perfectionist tendencies. Embrace the idea that tasks do not need to be perfect and focus on progress rather than flawless outcomes.

14. Develop a Growth Mindset:

- Cultivate a growth mindset that views challenges as opportunities for learning and improvement. Embrace setbacks as part of the learning process.

15. Seek Professional Support:

- If procrastination persists and significantly impacts your life, consider seeking support from a therapist or counselor. Professional guidance can help address underlying issues contributing to procrastination.

16. Practice Self-Compassion:

- Be kind to yourself when facing challenges. Acknowledge that everyone struggles at times and treat yourself with the same compassion you would offer a friend.

Breaking procrastination habits is a gradual process that involves consistent effort and commitment. Experiment with different strategies, be patient with yourself, and celebrate progress along the way. Remember, the goal is not perfection but continuous improvement and increased productivity.

CHAPTER SEVEN

From Procrastination to Triumph:
A Personal Success Story

In the fast-paced metropolis of London, a driven man named Alex discovered that he was a victim of persistent procrastination. Even with lofty objectives and aspirations, the propensity to put off work turned into a significant roadblock to achievement.

Alex was a gifted professional in the computer science industry who struggled with procrastination on a daily basis. Simple tasks would frequently be put off until the very last minute, which resulted in stress, lowered productivity, and lost chances.

He finally decided that enough was enough after observing the negative effects procrastination was having on both his personal and professional lives. This was the pivotal moment in his attempt to overcome his procrastination.

He started by making sure his goals were specific and doable. These objectives covered connections, relationships with others, and personal growth in addition to employment. A blueprint gave one a feeling of purpose and direction.

Recognising that big projects felt burdensome, Alex decided to divide them into smaller, more doable jobs. They were able to concentrate on taking one stride at a time using this strategy, gaining momentum gradually.

Alex integrated productive practices into his daily routine to fight procrastination. This includes creating a more ordered and efficient workspace, allocating specific time for concentrated work, and practicing mindfulness to remain in the present.

Although he was aware that failures were unavoidable, he chose to turn them into instructive opportunities. Every instance of procrastination provided a chance to review tactics, pinpoint triggers, and improve the strategy.

The adoption of a development mindset represented a significant change in Alex's viewpoint. Being able to see difficulties as chances for development and learning rather than as insurmountable hurdles encouraged perseverance and resilience. He had changed over time, and that was clear. Stress levels dropped, work quality increased, and both the professional and personal realms seemed more accomplished. Procrastination's unclimbable mountain had been defeated.

Alex is a living example of the transformational potential of conquering procrastination today. His success story is not just about reaching objectives; it's also about the personal development, resiliency, and confidence he gained by escaping the confines of procrastination.

Alex looks forward to a future full of unending growth, opportunities, and the satisfaction of knowing that they overcame procrastination to establish a life of purpose and fulfilment as the sun sets over the London cityscape.

CONCLUSION

The goal of conquering procrastination is a deep shift in one's perspective, routines, and way of living, not only the accomplishment of objectives. Alex's success story serves as an example of the significant positive effects that deliberate change may have on both one's personal and professional well-being.

Once a powerful foe, procrastination was defeated by tenacity and fortitude—the decision to pursue one's dreams without the burden of perpetual postponement. Anyone wishing to follow in Alex's footsteps might use his tactics—"setting clear goals, breaking down tasks, building a support system and embracing positive habits"—as a guide.

The path from procrastination to success is not without obstacles, disappointments, and epiphanies. It's about developing, learning, and acknowledging little accomplishments along the road. One can face the challenges of life with fresh vigour if they adopt a growth mentality and see barriers as opportunities rather than impediments.

Let Alex's success story inspire us and serve as a reminder that even in the face of firmly established habits, change is achievable. This story's ending marks the start of a new chapter full of possibilities, meaning, and the fulfilment that comes with living a life free from the constraints of procrastination.

I hope this narrative encourages others to start their own journeys of self-improvement, equipped with the conviction that they, too, can conquer procrastination and set of on a path towards a future full of achievements, fulfilment, and the delight of taking decisive action.

www.ingramcontent.com/pod-product-compliance
Lightning Source LLC
Chambersburg PA
CBHW071014290526
45795CB00005B/1801